Feelin

Written by Alison Hawes

Harcourt
Supplemental Publishers

Rigby • Steck-Vaughn

www.steck-vaughn.com

What Makes People Feel Happy?

I feel happy when Mom takes me to the park.
I like feeling happy.

I feel happy when I go swimming.
My sister feels happy, too.

What Makes People Feel Sad?

I feel sad when I can't go out to play.
I don't like feeling sad.

I feel sad when I fall down.
Even my friend feels sad.

What Makes People Feel Afraid?

I feel afraid when I am in the dark.
I don't like feeling afraid.

I feel afraid when I see a scary show.
Even my friends feel afraid!

What Makes People Feel Proud?

I feel proud when I do things by myself.
I like feeling proud.

I feel proud when I help Dad.
Dad feels proud of me, too.

What Makes People Feel Surprised?

I feel surprised when I get a gift.

I like feeling surprised.

I feel surprised when my gift barks at me!
Even my sister feels surprised!

What makes you feel surprised?